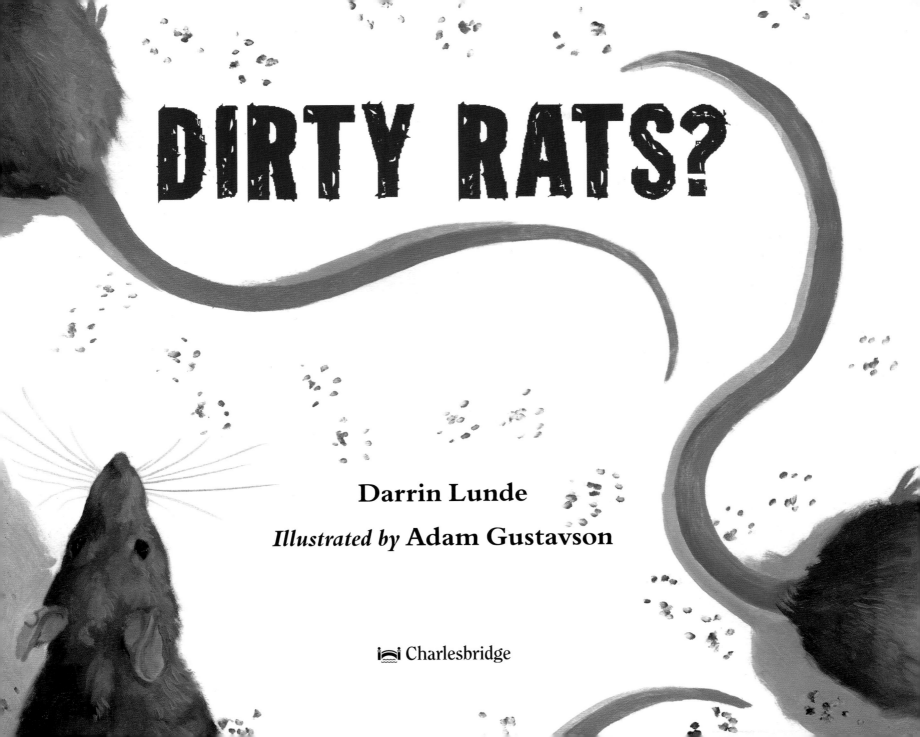

DIRTY RATS?

Darrin Lunde

Illustrated by **Adam Gustavson**

⌂ Charlesbridge

Dirty rats.

They eat garbage and live in sewers and subways.

Dirty rats.

They swarm and scurry in the night.

Dirty rats.

Their beady eyes and naked tails make us scream.
Eek! Aargh! Yikes!

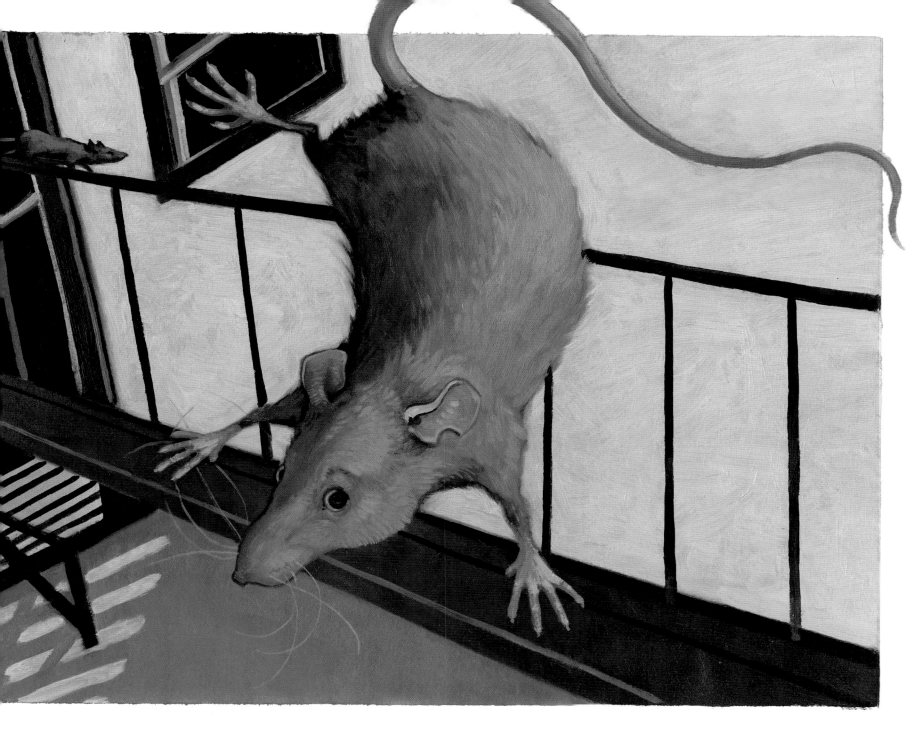

Dirty. Scary. Ugly.

Swat them! Trap them! Kill them!
But wait . . .

Not all rats eat garbage. The long-tailed marmoset rat eats only one kind of plant—bamboo. It feeds on bamboo fruit and flowers and nibbles on growing bamboo stems.

The long-tailed marmoset rat, *Hapalomys longicaudatus*, is an endangered species.
It lives in only a few lowland rain forests in Myanmar, Thailand, and Malaysia.
It makes its home by chewing a hole into a hollow bamboo stem.

Not all rats live in dirty sewer pipes. The South American fish-eating rat lives along clean mountain streams. It swims through the water, hunting for its next meal.

The fish-eating rat, *Anotomys leander,* lives only in northern Ecuador. Despite its name, it mostly eats insects. It uses its broad hind feet like flippers when swimming and has special muscles that close its ears to keep water out.

Not all rats scurry close to the ground. The banner-tailed kangaroo rat hops across desert grasslands. It has long hind legs and looks like a tiny kangaroo.

The banner-tailed kangaroo rat, *Dipodomys spectabilis*, lives in northern Mexico and the southwestern United States, where it digs complex burrows beneath large mounds of dirt. At full speed it can hop five or six feet at a time.

Not all rats have ugly, naked tails. The bushy-tailed cloud rat's tail is completely covered in fur.

The bushy-tailed cloud rat, *Crateromys schadenbergi*, is an endangered species that lives in the mountain forests of the northern Philippines. It is the size of a large house cat, lives high up in trees, and is active only at night.

Rats can even help humans. Scientists study laboratory rats to understand why we get sick. These rats help millions of people stay healthy.

White lab rats are a type of *Rattus norvegicus* that has been bred for medical research. Scientists hope this research will prevent future suffering. Thanks to laboratory rats, we have learned about heart disease, nerve damage, diabetes, and other health problems.

Rats help plants spread their seeds. Without rats many kinds of plants and trees would not grow.

Rats like to eat seeds, but they may also take them away and bury them in a process called scatter hoarding. If the seeds aren't retrieved, they grow into new plants.

Rats are food for many predators. Emerald tree boas, burrowing owls, and servals could not live without rats.

Wild animals hunt and eat millions of rats every day. Rats reproduce quickly, so there are always plenty to eat.

Rats are hated, hunted, trapped, and feared.
They struggle each day just to survive.

Most rats die before their first birthday, and three years is about the longest most rats live in the wild.

Dirty rats?

Maybe.
Maybe not.

Other Rats

Cricetomys species

African giant pouched rats (two species in the genus *Cricetomys*) are quite gentle. They have such a good sense of smell that they are used by demolition experts to locate explosives in minefields.

Josephoartigasia monesi

Though not true rats, the largest rodents that ever lived, *Josephoartigasia monesi*, made their home in South America about three million years ago. Scientists estimate that they weighed as much as three thousand pounds, which is about the weight of an adult rhinoceros.

Lophiomys imhausi

Crested rats, *Lophiomys imhausi*, live in East Africa and are the world's only poisonous rats. They gnaw and chew the roots and bark of a particular poisonous tree and then slobber the poison onto special absorbent hairs along their sides. Once filled with poison, these hairs can be deadly to the touch.

Hundreds of rat species are known to exist in the world today, and new species are discovered every year.

Mallomys **species**

The largest rats today are the woolly rats (various species of the genus *Mallomys*), which live in New Guinea. From the tip of their nose to the tip of their tail, they can measure up to eighteen inches long.

Neotoma **species**

Pack rats (various species of the genus *Neotoma*), live throughout North America and are infamous thieves. They build large nests by gathering up sticks, bones, and other debris. They are especially fond of small shiny objects and have been known to steal spoons, keys, coins, and watches.

Psammomys obesus

Fat sand rats, *Psammomys obesus*, live in the Sahara Desert. They have the unusual habit of communicating with one another by loudly tapping their feet.

Learn More About Rats

The definitive reference that scientists use to keep track of all mammal species (including rats) is *Mammal Species of the World*, edited by Don E. Wilson and DeeAnn M. Reeder. The entire book is available online.
www.bucknell.edu/msw3/

For information on the conservation status of any mammal, visit the International Union for Conservation of Nature's Red List of Threatened Species.
www.iucnredlist.org

The American Society of Mammalogists is one of the most important professional societies for people who study mammals. A number of relevant resources are available on the organization's website.
www.mammalsociety.org

In addition to displaying animals in their exhibit halls, natural history museums preserve many thousands more specimens behind the scenes. These specimens are kept for scientists, and they include the remains of all known species. Scientists make important discoveries using these collections.

Some of the largest natural history collections include the American Museum of Natural History in New York City; the National Museum of Natural History in Washington, DC; the Field Museum of Natural History in Chicago; the Natural History Museum of Los Angeles County in California; and the Natural History Museum in London. There are also many more smaller museums in major cities and universities around the world.

Many zoos recognize the popularity of rats, and there are some excellent species on exhibit at the Smithsonian's National Zoo in Washington, DC; the Bronx Zoo in New York City; the San Diego Zoo; the Philadelphia Zoo; and the Columbus Zoo and Aquarium.

For my lovely wife, Sakiko—D. L.

For Andy and Pete, of course—A. G.

Text copyright © 2015 by Darrin Lunde
Illustrations copyright © 2015 by Adam Gustavson
All rights reserved, including the right of reproduction in whole or in part in any form.
Charlesbridge and colophon are registered trademarks of Charlesbridge Publishing, Inc.

Published by Charlesbridge
85 Main Street
Watertown, MA 02472
(617) 926-0329
www.charlesbridge.com

Library of Congress Cataloging-in-Publication Data
Lunde, Darrin P., author.
    Dirty rats?/Darrin Lunde; illustrated by Adam Gustavson.
        pages cm
    ISBN 978-1-58089-566-8 (reinforced for library use)
    ISBN 978-1-60734-759-0 (ebook)
    ISBN 978-1-60734-623-4 (ebook pdf)
1. Rattus—Juvenile literature. 2. Rats—Juvenile literature.
I. Gustavson, Adam, illustrator. II. Title.
QL737.R666L86 2015
599.35—dc23   2013049022

Printed in China
(hc) 10 9 8 7 6 5 4 3 2 1

Illustrations done in oil on prepared Rives BFK printmaking paper
Display type set in Tuzonie by HBI at Aah Yes Fonts
Text type set in Aldine 401 BT by Bitstream, Inc.
Color separations by KHL Chroma Graphics, Singapore
Printed by Jade Productions in Heyuan, Guangdong, China
Production supervision by Brian G. Walker
Designed by Martha MacLeod Sikkema